SIOUX WOMEN

VIRGINIA DRIVING HAWK SNEVE

SIOUX WOMEN

TRADITIONALLY SACRED

SOUTH

DAKOTA

HISTORICAL

SOCIETY

PRESS

Pierre

This publication is
funded, in part, by the
Great Plains Education
Foundation, Inc.,
Aberdeen, S.Dak.

Library of Congress Cataloging-in-Publication data
[Names: Sneve, Virginia Driving Hawk, author.
Title: Sioux women : traditionally sacred / Virginia Driving Hawk Sneve.
Description: Pierre, SD : South Dakota Historical Society Press, [2016] |
    Includes bibliographical references and index. | Audience: Ages 13-16.
Identifiers: LCCN 2016026182 | ISBN 9781941813072 (alk. paper)
Subjects: LCSH: Dakota women—Juvenile literature. | Dakota
    Indians—History—Juvenile literature. | Dakota Indians—Social life and
    customs—Juvenile literature.
Classification: LCC E99.D1 S61813 2016 | DDC 978.004/975243—dc23 LC record
available at https://lccn.loc.gov/2016026182

The paper in this book meets the guidelines for permanence
and durability of the Committee on Production Guidelines for
Book Longevity of the Council on Library Resources.

Cover image: Portrait of four American Indian women wearing European American
clothing and bonnets. *South Dakota State Historical Society*

Frontispiece: A Sioux matriarch with two granddaughters, 1948.
South Dakota State Historical Society

Text and cover design by Rich Hendel

Please visit our website at sdhspress.com.

Printed in the United States of America

20 19 18 17 16   1 2 3 4 5

For all women of the Sioux nation

CONTENTS

Introduction / 1

1 WOMEN'S ROLE / 3

2 WINTER COUNTS AND CHANGING TIMES / 21

3 RESERVATION AND SCHOOL / 29

4 WOMEN ADAPT / 51

5 THE CIRCLE NEVER ENDS / 73

Notes / 89

Sources / 93

Index / 97

SIOUX WOMEN

On April 13, 2007, the South Dakota State Historical Society held its annual history conference; the title was "Romancing the West: Women's Lives on the Great Plains." Scholars gave papers on immigrant women, women in politics, Calamity Jane and other women of South Dakota; I did a Power-Point presentation called "American Indian Women."

In that paper, I focused on the American Indian women of South Dakota. Later, Nancy Tystad Koupal, director of the Research and Publishing Program of the historical society, asked me to write a book about Lakota women. I agreed, but I found that I had to expand the topic to more than "Lakota."

French explorers and Christian missionaries first encountered the Ojibwa tribe, whose members told of an enemy tribe, the *Nadewesiou*, which meant "treacherous snake." The French took the last part of the name, and we became "Sioux." However, our name for ourselves is Dakota, Nakota, Lakota. In this work, I will refer to these tribes as Sioux because not one of the three names is inclusive of all the subtribes that make up this Indian nation. I will also refer to the tribes collectively as American Indians.

This book is not an academic study of American Indian women, but it is the result of my interest in exploring female lives as experienced by Sioux women. In 1985, I presented a paper, "The Women of the Circle," at the Nordland Fest at Augustana College, Sioux Falls, South Dakota. The circle is an important concept to the Sioux; it is a sacred symbol of life: people are born and they live within the circle of family, tribe, and nation. What one person or creature does affects all others within the circle. The cycle of life repeats itself, just as the circle never ends. Women are the center of that circle, caring for family and acting for community.

The author (left) around age sixteen, with grandmother Hannah Frazier, grandmother Harriet Ross, and mother Rose Driving Hawk Posey. *Virginia Driving Hawk Sneve Collection*

I have written of Sioux women in books and other articles in addition to the presentations noted above; much of this present work comes from those previous articles or books. This book is not a compilation of biographical sketches of individual women, but I do use specific women to illustrate points in the story and identify them by tribal affiliation.

In the introduction to my book *Completing the Circle*, I wrote of how my grandmother taught me to make a star quilt and of what making a quilt means to me: "As I fashion a quilt, it reminds me of life formed about a youthful core of pulsing hopes and bright dreams that broaden to multihued circles of womanhood. The circle widens until the blended hues narrow to a single-colored point of the star that is life's end. Just as the diamond pieces are joined, so is my life bound to the lives of my mother and grandmothers." This experience led me to explore American Indian women's lives as experienced by my Sioux grandmothers and other female relatives whom I interviewed for *Circle*.

Sioux Women: Traditionally Sacred continues that search, but my interests have widened to include concerns about contemporary American Indian girls and women's struggles to maintain traditional values in the modern world.

The Sioux tribe consists of three major divisions: Santee, Teton, and Yankton. French explorer Pierre Radisson met the Santee in 1660 when they resided near the lakes and woods of the upper Mississippi River. They were the mother tribe, who called themselves Dakota. One branch split and ranged across the northern plains from the Missouri River to the Rockies and became the Teton. A smaller group, the Yankton, inhabited the region between the other two. The three groups also had dialectic variations in language. The Santee spoke Dakota, the Yankton, Nakota, and the Teton, Lakota; all mean "allies," or an alliance of friends.

Radisson reported that the Sioux women seemed to be drudges who attended to all chores while the men hunted and fished. His judgment came from the point of view of the upper class European tradition, in which women did little physical work and hunting and fishing were leisure-time pursuits. In that culture, women were subservient to men.

Radisson did not understand that the Indian woman's work was essential to the tribe's well being and survival just as much as the man's hunting, which provided meat, and his skills as a warrior, which protected the women, children, and elders. The Frenchmen and other explorers and missionaries disparaged Indian women's work, and they did not know of the White Buffalo Calf Woman who gave directions to all the people about how they should conduct their lives.

The Sioux believe that the story, now called a legend, was the basis for the tribe's social and spiritual values. I tell this story as my grandmother, Flora Driving Hawk, related it when I was a young girl sitting by her side on summer evenings.

Somewhere over by the Pipestone Quarries, the people met to pray to Wakantanka. Two young men went to hunt in order to feed the many people. They walked until there was a bright light in front of them. In the middle of the bright light was a beautiful young girl all dressed in white.

"I am from the Buffalo People," she said. "They sent me to talk to your people. Go to them and tell them I am coming and to prepare a council tipi for me."

She was so beautiful that one of the young men wanted to make love to her. He tried to grab her and throw her down. The other man warned, "Don't!"

But it was too late. There was a crash of thunder, and a big cloud and lightning surrounded him and the girl. When it cleared, the man was a crisp skeleton on the ground. (Ever since that time, the White Buffalo Calf Woman protects girls from bad men.)

The other man trembled and could not look at the woman. But she said, "Don't be afraid. I will not harm you. Now go to your people."

He ran to the village and told the people what had happened and what they must do. They were all excited and rushed to get everything ready. Soon from the east with the sunrise she came, all dressed in white and so beautiful. She carried a bundle and walked to the council tipi with its door to the east (which is why tipis are always set up that way).

She entered and turned to the left (which is why that is the women's side). She sat and placed her legs to the right side and tucked her feet in (which is why women always sit that way).

When she spoke in a soft gentle voice (which is why women should never be loud), all were quiet to hear her (which is why no one should speak while someone else is). Everyone understood her, but the words she used were different from the way the men spoke (which is why women have a special way of talking).

She told the people about Wakantanka and told them that she was their sister. She opened her bundle, and there was a polished red stone pipe. She presented it to the sky, earth, and the four corners. "See the sacred pipe," she said as she held it before them. "Use it only for peace and never for war."

"My sisters," she addressed the women. "You have hard things to do in your life. You have pain when you have babies, and it is difficult to raise children. But you are important because without you there would be no people. So, you will have babies for your husband. You take the buffalo he brings home, cook it for him

Flora Driving Hawk, ca. 1970. *Virginia Driving Hawk Sneve Collection*

and your children; make clothes and build tipis, and all in the tipis will belong to you—even the children. You will be good wives
and mothers."

Then she spoke to the young unmarried girls. "You will not lie
with a man until you get married, and you will always be faithful
to your husband."

Then she talked to the men. "My brothers," she called them,
"you must have good thoughts about girls so that they will be
pure when they marry. When you take wives (because she said
'wives,' men could have more than one), be kind to all of them.
She told them to be good to the children and all elders (which is
why there are no orphans, and old ones are respected and taken
care of until they die).

She stayed with the people four days and taught them how
to use the pipe for healing and in seven sacred ceremonies. She
turned and left, walking back to the east. As she went, she turned
into a white buffalo calf (which is why no one kills a white buffalo calf). She was a sacred woman and because of her, all Sioux
women are sacred.[1]

A modern Sioux artist talking about the importance of buffalo
to his culture noted, "*Tatanka* is the male buffalo, and *pte* is the
female. . . . Our society is a matriarchal society. When you see
a herd of buffalo, a female is in the lead. That's the way it is in
our culture, as well: A grandmother or an aunt is the one in the
family who makes the decisions."[2] Elderly women are still highly
respected in Sioux culture, and their decisions are honored because they usually know what is best for their families.

The Sioux, who had no written language, passed on the important aspects of tribal life by "telling," which has become
known as the oral tradition. Grandmothers were often the oral
historians who told the White Buffalo Calf Woman story with individual variation so that there is not one "correct" telling. Later,
researchers collected Sioux legends and recorded the tale in written form.[3]

(*opposite*)
Sioux woman and
child on a traditional
cradleboard. *South
Dakota State Historical
Society*

Young girl wearing a
quill-decorated yoke,
leggings, and moccasins,
1898. *South Dakota State
Historical Society*

Another tale tells of an aged, nameless woman. Again, I tell
the story as my grandmother told it to me. They say that an old
woman and her dog live out in the Badlands. She sits on the
ground with little piles of colored porcupine quills spread on a
hide. She is decorating a robe with a pretty quillwork design. She
gets tired sitting like that, so every so often she has to get up to
stretch. Sometimes when she gets up she goes to fix the fire so it

won't go out. All the while, the dog watches her. When she is busy fixing the fire, the dog gets up—he stretches, too—then goes to the robe and pulls out the quill. This way, the work is never finished. If the woman ever finishes her quillwork, it will be the end of the world.

Quillwork was a beautiful craft among Sioux women, and legend tells that it was Anog Ite, Double-Faced Woman, who introduced it. She was the daughter of Skan, the spirit of the sky, and wife to Tate, the wind. She was beautiful, but vain about her looks. She was a restless girl, sometimes a proper wife, but she acted impulsively. She often disobeyed her father and husband who told her to stay at home, and she wandered about the universe. On one of these treks she was attracted to Wi, the Sun God, and she tried to seduce him so that she could take the place of his wife, Hanwi, the moon. Anog Ite's husband, Tate, was heart-broken, and Hanwi hid her face in shame. This is why the moon goes through the different phases during the month; she hides her face in shame.

Skan punished Anog Ite by giving her a second, hideous face. Her two faces are symbols of disharmony and dissension. When a girl misbehaves, her mother might caution her to be good or she would have to go outside where Anog Ite might grab her. The beautiful face would calm a child's fears, but the ugly face would spank the child.

Among the Sioux, parents warn young women not to be like Anog Ite, but the story beguiles them, and they dream of her. In some dreams, she teaches the dreamer how to quill. These gifted women are loners, spending most of their time perfecting their craft, and they prefer the company of other women. Some become lesbians, and as such, their lives have two sides, happiness with another woman, but sorrow because they will not have children.

When I was a little girl, a couple came to church in a horse-pulled wagon. They were both about the same size, rather slight

Woman decorating a moccasin top with porcupine quills. *South Dakota State Historical Society*

and quiet. One wore what had become a traditional woman's dress, high-necked cotton calico with moccasins and a shawl about her head and shoulders. The other had on black trousers and jacket, cowboy boots, and a black hat. As was the custom, the one dressed as a woman sat with the women on one side of the church, and the other sat on the men's side. They were both women, but the congregation accepted them and did not shun them. The woman did quillwork.

It is through such legends as the White Buffalo Calf Woman and Anog Ite that we learn the nature of the nomadic Sioux, but we must go to oral history to discover how women actually fared during that time. I was fortunate in knowing grandmothers who told me of family history, and I wrote that in the book *Completing the Circle*. Earlier writers also contributed to our understanding of the past by sharing their families' stories. Luther Standing Bear, for example, learned to read and write English at Carlisle Indian School in Pennsylvania. In his autobiography, *My People the Sioux*, published in 1928, he recorded prereservation life and

Luther Standing Bear
(standing, middle) with
two visiting chiefs and a
group of Carlisle Indian
School students, 1879.
*National Anthropological
Archives, Smithsonian
Institution*

told of his mother Pretty Face, who was the most beautiful young woman among the Sioux at the time she married his father.

Standing Bear relates a story of his mother's bravery. She heard warriors tell of how they were on their way back to camp and they stopped at a railroad station to ask for water. The agent refused, which angered the warriors, who were going to take revenge. Pretty Face took an axe and followed them to the tracks. She chopped the ties into pieces so that the men could remove them. They waited until the train came and its crew fired on them. The whites laughed as the Indians gave chase, and they did not notice the broken space on the track; the train derailed and crashed. Pretty Face ran to the overturned cars and carried away what she could of sugar and cloth. "My mother obtained from this train wreck the first beads ever seen by the Sioux Nation," Standing Bear wrote, and he credited her as the first to use the brightly colored beads in place of the labor-intensive porcupine quills. She sewed beads onto a buffalo skin, and her son claimed to be the first Sioux to wear beads on a blanket around his body.[4]

Standing Bear went on to recall how his mother and other women engaged in the labor of preparing buffalo hides for tipis and the making of tipis. They decorated the tipis with individual designs and painted or beaded all of the accessories within them and all of the clothing.[5] It was done with great respect for the beast that had enriched the Indians' lives.

The buffalo played an important role for the Sioux. Scholar Marla Powers noted that there was always a relationship in ceremonies between males and females (buffalo bulls and buffalo cows). The rites emphasized sexual reproduction as well as the people's reliance on the buffalo for food. Women and buffalo were associated with creating and sustaining life. The sexual nature of the initiation ceremonies is important because these rites symbolically transformed an individual into a male or a female.

Monthly, as long as she menstruated, each young woman went to a lone tipi, where her female relatives cared for her and told her to rest and practice her quillwork and other crafts. She was forbidden to cook. She must avoid men and their weapons because a menstruating woman could make them impotent.

A young woman also received lessons in chastity. Her mother tied a rawhide belt about her and made her sleep in a leather bag that protected her from men so that she would remain chaste until she married. Even so, a man would crawl along the outside of the tipi until he found the site of the sleeping girl. He quietly pulled up a picket and tried to creep into the girl's bed. But he was most often heard by the girl's mother, who chased him away. The women called him "tipi crawler," and he was often the butt of jokes from his friends.[6]

Madonna Swan, 1946.
University of Oklahoma Press

Madonna Swan, born in 1928, told her recollections of three generations of the women in her family to Mark St. Pierre in *Madonna Swan: A Lakota Woman's Story* (1991). Swan recalled her first menstruation:

Mom and Grandma closed off a little space for me to stay with ropes and blankets, . . . where Grandma said I must stay for the next four days and four nights. Grandma Julia instructed me not to look out the windows [or door]. . . . "You are to stay busy doing something all the time; . . . you should be sewing or beading. . . . [If] you make a mistake, you should not rip it out. If you do, you will be that way the rest of your life. . . . So just keep going and the next time do it better," she instructed. . . . Grandma told me, "Within these days you are not to have a bad disposition or think bad thoughts about anyone or anything. Try to be happy and not to get angry or else that will also be your way in life." She told me not to scratch my head or itch myself anywhere.[7]

Each day, Swan's mother and grandmother bathed her and prayed for her: "Grandfathers above and in the four directions, make Madonna a good woman. Help her to treat guests with hospitality. Grandfathers, help her to be a good worker. Grandfathers, and Maka Ina (Mother Earth), help Madonna to be a good mother. I pray that the food she cooks in her life will be good for those that eat it. Grandfathers, help her to be a good wife and live with the same man all her life. Grandfathers, bless her with healthy children." Madonna's grandmother also taught her to be thankful to the Great Spirit for what he had given to and done for the people. She was to thank him for health and to pray when in trouble or in need to the four directions and to Hanwi, the Moon, Tate, the wind, and "Whope, the beautiful one," who is the White Buffalo Calf Woman who brought the sacred pipe.[8]

After four days, Madonna went back to her normal life, and her family made a feast and gave away the items they had prepared for this day and those she had made in her isolation. She was a young woman now, and she could no longer climb trees or play with boys as she used to do.[9] She must respect her brothers and not shame her family.

My grandmothers also recalled the instruction they received at their first menses: "It wasn't like it used to be. We didn't have to go off by ourselves until we stopped bleeding, but we had to keep our bodies clean and our thoughts pure. We were told that we were women now; we could now have babies, but not until after we had a husband." Girls often received traditional instructions in proper behavior at a formal Buffalo Ceremony following their first menses:

> The spider is an industrious woman.
> She builds a tepee for her children
> and feeds them well.
> The turtle is a wise woman.
> She hears many things
> and saves them for her children.
> Her skin is a shield,
> An arrow cannot wound her.
> The lark is a cheerful woman.
> She brings pleasant weather
> to her lodge.
> She does not scold.
> She is always happy.[10]

After the initiation ceremony, a young woman was ready for marriage. She may have already had her eye on a young man and he on her, but until her menses, it could mean nothing. After the ceremony that the medicine man held to honor her, the whole village was aware of her status.

As adults, some women became medicine women. My great

Flora Driving Hawk,
age eighteen. *Virginia
Driving Hawk Sneve
Collection*

grandmother, Pejuta Okawin, was such a person, but she did not practice formal rituals as the men did. She knew of many natural medicines and treated illnesses and injuries.

Once a girl attained adult status, a suitor could formally woo her. My grandmothers recalled how courting was done. At night when all were asleep, the young man stood outside the girl's tipi and played a plaintive love song on his flute. She quietly slipped out of the tipi while her parents slept (or pretended to). She took her robe with her and invited him to stand within its warmth with his arms about her.

My grandmother Flora Driving Hawk recalled that at boarding school her young suitor used this courting method. "He had no flute to play," she recalled, "but Robert told his friend to tell his sister to tell me to come out of the dorm that night and I did. We stood in my blanket and he gave me an apple. But we got caught, and even though we had done nothing (no sex) we were expelled," she told me years later. Flora was heartbroken and reluctantly went home to her father, who scolded her for shaming the family. But Robert came for her and "Everything was all right."

Robert Driving Hawk had gone back to the Lower Brule reservation and worked hard for his uncle to save money to build a house—then he went to get Flora. Even though he surprised her, she packed her few belongings and went home with him. "We stopped at the [Rosebud] Agency to get married at the Episcopal Church and then traveled to Lower Brule and lived in the house he had built for me," Grandma recalled.

In the era before reservations, girls respected and cared for the men in their lives and supported them in times of war. Women sent the warriors off with shrill, trilling cries and welcomed them home in the same way. Women also trilled to mourn the dead or to celebrate a happy event. This cry is still used at powwows, weddings, graduations, and funerals to express joy and/or sorrow.

Warfare was an accepted fact of life for the Sioux. Women belonged to warrior societies in groups that today we might call

Mary Crawler,
also known as
Moving Robe
Woman. *National
Anthropological
Archives, Smithsonian
Institution*

auxiliaries. For example, among the Lakota, women served as singers in the *Tokala* ("Fox") and *Cante T'inza* ("Strong Heart") societies. In the dances of the *Napešni* ("No Flight") societies, the male members of which wore long sashes that were staked to the ground during a fight, the sisters of such warriors joined in the circular dance holding on to their brother's sashes.[11]

Some women actually participated in battles, and Moving Robe Woman, a Hunkapa also known as Mary Crawler, told of her experiences in the Battle of the Little Bighorn. Moving Robe Woman was digging turnips with other girls when she saw a cloud of dust and heard a warrior shout that soldiers were coming. She ran to her tipi, where she learned that her brother had been killed. She painted her face, braided her hair, and rode her horse into battle. "I was not afraid," she said. Moving Robe Woman said that it was Pehin Hanska (Long Hair, George Armstrong Custer) attacking the village.[12] She rode holding her brother's staff, and Rain-in-the-Face was so impressed that he shouted to the men that they should not hide behind her skirts as they raced to the river to trap Custer's men.[13] As noted earlier, a girl must behave properly and not bring shame to herself or her family. She must respect her brothers and male cousins, but Moving Robe Woman physically joined the warriors and honored her dead brother by taking his place in battle.

Almost a century later, women were present to support the men in the 1970s when the American Indian Movement (AIM) occupied the village of Wounded Knee. One, Mary Crow Dog, joined AIM at age eighteen. She participated in AIM's protest in the 1972 Trail of Broken Treaties and the occupation of the Bureau of Indian Affairs (BIA) headquarters in Washington, D.C. During the occupation of Wounded Knee, she gave birth to her first child. Two medicine men honored her for her bravery and gave her the name Ohitika Win (Brave Woman). The occupation was a militant demonstration that attracted international attention to the American Indian's dismal plight on America's Indian reservations.

Mary Crow Dog's book *Lakota Woman*, published in 1990 and edited by Richard Erdoes, told of her life until 1977 and won the 1991 American Book Award. Erdoes also edited her second book, *Ohitika Woman,* which continued her life story. *Lakota Woman,* a made for TV film, depicted the events of AIM's occupation at Wounded Knee.[14] We now find information about Moving Robe Woman and other American Indian women in such records. Before that, the winter count used pictographic images to record our history.

Winter Counts were a prewriting way of recording a tribe's history that augmented the oral tradition. The historian, sometimes called the keeper of the winter count, drew pictographic symbols to represent an event for each particular year. Scholars now date the counts by known events common to all nations, that is, epidemics, floods, comets, and the arrival of Europeans.

In my study of three winter counts of the Western Sioux, I found few events concerning women—only twenty-one examples in 181 years. Some of these events recorded general misfortunes that befell women, such as the event selected for 1799, "many women died in childbirth." Others depicted women involved in suicide and violence, such as these examples from the Big Missouri winter count now located at the Journey Museum in Rapid City, South Dakota:

1799 pictograph, Big Missouri Winter Count.

1828, an abused woman fled to her father. Her husband pursued her, attacked the father, and took her back to his tipi. The father followed and killed him.

1838, a man from Broken Bow's camp stole a wife from another camp. This caused a bad feeling and the man was killed.

Sam Kills Two working on the Big Missouri Winter Count.
Nebraska State Historical Society

 1857, a Crow woman was
killed by the Sioux.

 1883, Dog Shield died.
His grieving wife hanged herself.
They were buried together.[1]

The records of women in winter counts indicate that they did commit suicide but that they rarely were killed. Only later, on the reservations, did murder of both sexes and all ages become a frequent crime. Written records of the fur-trade era show that a husband punished an unfaithful wife by shaving her head from the nape of the neck to the brow, mutilating her arms and hands, and slashing her shoulder blades.

Unfaithful men did not suffer the same public humiliation; indeed, a man was thought to be more manly if he successfully seduced another's wife. However, if the husband's philandering became so blatant as to cause embarrassment and shame to the wife's family, she could leave him and take the children with her. She might also take after him with a knife or an axe, and often her brothers would trap him coming from his lover's house and beat him.

The winter counts show only a brief glimpse of the culture and life that Sioux women knew until it all changed with the coming of fur traders who took Indian women as wives. French traders came from Canada or Saint Louis, Missouri, and one man might have a wife in each of several tribes with whom he traded. He might also have married sisters or have many wives in one band. Spanish and Anglo-Saxon traders also sired children by Indian women. These liaisons were a mixed blessing, bringing many

new and useful goods to the tribes but also some new products, customs, and diseases that proved disastrous.[2]

The first Sioux women who cohabited with white men brought honor to their families. But they soon found that their lives were filled with drudgery if there were no "sister-wives" to share the household work and conjugal duties. A single wife gave birth more frequently and over a longer period of time. As a result, she suffered more from childbirth.

By the 1850s, the tribes were distrustful of the whites, and a woman married to a white man found her status lowered. Frequently, she lived apart from her nomadic family. She had no father or brothers to protect her, and if she ran to her father's house, he often denied admission into the family circle. The most difficult thing for her to accept was the fact that all the goods in her non-Indian household were the property of the man. She had lost control of her home and of her children.

The fur trade also led to general deterioration of the female's status as Indian husbands began bartering pelts that their wives had tanned for guns and whiskey. At Fort Laramie in Wyoming Territory, where important treaties were signed in the 1860s, the Indian relatives of women married to traders became dependent on trade goods and whiskey. They no longer hunted to supply food or shelter for their families. These Indians, called "fort Indians," or *waglukhe*, became known as the "Loafer band." The Brule called them "hang-around-the-fort Indians."[3]

After the decline of the fur trade, many traders stayed with their Indian wives and children, but many more returned to their original homes. Others abandoned wives and children or, leaving the wife, raised the children as whites. Some traders took only the male children or sent them back East to be educated, but as adults, these sons often returned to their mothers' tribes to live as Indians.

As more fur traders and settlers moved west, the United States military began to have a strong presence on the upper Great

(*opposite*)
Ceremonial tipi depicting events in Sioux history, ca. 1895. *Nebraska State Historical Society*

Plains. The Sioux and other tribes were in the way of white settlement and had to be removed and confined. The Sioux fought back, and their most dramatic win came at the Battle of the Little Bighorn in 1876. Moving Robe Woman, mentioned earlier, took part in the fight, replacing her brother on the battlefield. Other women did not fight, but they went among the enemy dead and mutilated their bodies, possibly as revenge for wrongs done to them or to keep the men from doing battle in the next world. The military presence in the West resulted in large numbers of fatherless, mixed-race children born because of the alcohol trade, prostitution, or rape during and after military engagements.

The celebration of victory following the Battle of the Little Bighorn was short lived. The tribes scattered in many directions, knowing that the United States Army would pursue them. The tribes were rounded up; their guns, horses, and tipis were taken or destroyed; and the people were confined on reservations. On March 2, 1889 (the same year South and North Dakota became states), Congress passed an act that divided the Great Sioux Reservation, which had covered the area of the western half of present-day South Dakota, into five smaller reservations.

Confinement destroyed the Sioux male's lifestyle as warrior and hunter, leaving him aimless in the new life. The government allotted each adult 160 acres of land, which the males were expected to farm. But farming had been women's work in the old life, and it was not until the next generation that most Sioux men began to farm and ranch. Female lives did not change as much on the reservations; women quickly adapted to the new life. A wife no longer had to tan hides for lodging or clothing, but she still cared for her family as she always had. Now they lived in extended family villages called *tiyospayes*.

The people adopted white-style clothing because they no longer had access to the game animals that had fed and clothed them. The men wore woven trousers and shirts and favored the black reservation hat; yet, they still preferred moccasins to hard

Sioux women cook together by Rosebud Creek.
South Dakota State Historical Society

shoes. Women wore leggings and moccasins on which they worked quill or bead designs, but their ankle–length gowns were of calico, not leather.

Missionaries had been among the Dakotas since Father Louis Hennepin visited them in 1680. In the West, Jesuit missionary Father Pierre De Smet traveled the Missouri River baptizing children and adults in the 1840s. Women converted more easily to Christianity than men because, again, their role as wife and mother did not change. Much more was required of a male when he converted. He could have only one wife; he must cut his hair, wear pants rather than a breechcloth, and farm.

However, some women also suffered from Christianity. Prior to the new religion, single women were a rarity in tribal societies. Now, on the reservation, a man could only have one wife, and the other(s) had to be set aside. A woman who was put aside often had to struggle to raise her children if she had no brother or some other relative to give her family a home. The new farmers often barely eked out an existence and were dependent on government rations to survive. Single women and their children were too often a burden that they could not support. Nor was there room in single-family cabins; the days of being able to provide another tipi to a growing family were no more.⁴

Unmarried Indian women became objects of pity and scorn. They resorted to prostitution and abandoned their children, who often were sent to boarding schools because grandparents, dependent on government housing and food rationing, could not take them. However, most parents were unwilling to send their children to the agency boarding schools, because often they did not see them again until the children finished school, which might be as long as five years.

My grandmothers were the first generation to be born on a reservation, and their parents lived on allotted reservation lands. In 1887, the federal government passed the Dawes, or General Allotment, Act, which divided the reservation into small allotments of 160 acres and assigned them to individual Indians registered on the tribal rolls.[1] Many Sioux women moved from a tipi to a log house on their own or their husbands' land. They learned to cook on an iron stove and wear white clothing. Children had to go to school, even though the parents did not want to send them.

Agents of the Bureau of Indian Affairs (BIA), who managed all reservation affairs, threatened to arrest parents or withhold food rations unless the children attended school. As a result, the next generation of Sioux women were educated in schools run by European Americans. Bdi Bdi Win, Evelyn Dumarce Crawford of Sisseton, told that her grandmother kept her hidden from BIA officials until they threatened to put her grandparents in jail. Bdi, as she was nicknamed, started school at nine years of age, when she got the name Evelyn.[2]

Like Bdi, my grandmothers adapted to school, just as their mothers had adapted to living in log cabins. However, the white educators did not understand the traditional freedom that the Indians had granted their young nor that Sioux education had been by precept and example. There were thus clashes between old and new values. Teachers found it difficult to discipline children who were not used to any kind of control.

The intricacies of the Sioux kinship system and its duties, which had held the tribes together, further complicated the lives of students. Illness or trouble in the family often led students to

Teacher Thisbe
Hutson (in hat)
with students at the
boarding school on
the Pine Ridge Indian
Reservation, July 1890.
*South Dakota State
Historical Society*

leave the campus to help at home. When students left for vaca-tion, they returned when they thought it was time and not when the calendar said it was time. The teachers did not understand the Sioux's concept of time and duty—all was done when the time was right to benefit family and *tiyospaye*.[3]

Linguistic peculiarities also created problems. Sioux anthro-pologist Ella Deloria explained:

> "You won't do that again, will you?" asked a teacher, correct-ing a child. "Yes," said the child each time the question was re-peated. "Well, of all perversity!" thought the teacher. . . . But the trouble was that in Dakota you say "yes" to a question like that, when in English you say "no." English says, "No (I will not)." Dakota says, "Yes (you are right that I will not)."[4]

The children were confused, but they did as the teacher asked.

Ella Deloria, right.
Virginia Driving Hawk
Sneve Collection

Soon their days were a repetitive routine. Children did chores according to their age. Older girls rose early in the morning to prepare breakfast for the whole school. They learned to make oatmeal and serve it with molasses and coffee. The girls sat apart from the boys, and a teacher sat at the head of the table.

Each child had to drink milk with each meal. The white staff knew it was a healthy and cheap source of protein when there was little meat available. However, children's digestion reacted with diarrhea until their systems became accustomed to the foreign drink. My Grandma Flora giggled when she told of the "stinky slop pails in the dorm" that were used during the night when the children could not go out to the privies. She giggled more when telling me of the gas they all had from the milk even when they did not have diarrhea anymore. The teachers admonished them to say, "Pardon me," after a child farted and to try not to laugh. No one knew about lactose intolerance, which is still an issue among American Indians.

Older girls worked in the laundry, and the stronger boys hauled water to fill the copper boilers on the stoves, which they stoked with wood. The girls dumped the soiled clothing into the boil-

Laundry room,
Flandreau Indian
School. *South Dakota*
State Historical Society

ers filled with harsh lye soap. They lifted the heavy, wet, steaming laundry into cold tubs of water, swirled it around, and then lifted and wrung it out with theirs hands. Girls hung the damp clothing and bedding outdoors on long lines to blow dry in the ever-present prairie wind. In the winter, the laundry froze into grotesque forms that frightened the little children. The older girls gathered the clothes and hefted heavy sad irons heated to red heat and pressed out the wrinkles. The smaller children did not have as physically demanding chores. Boys helped tote wood to fires, and little girls carried the clean clothes to the dorms.

As they often worked together without supervision, the children spoke Dakota or Lakota to each other without fear of punishment for "talking Indian," their native language. At all other times, they had to speak English. In classrooms, boys sat on one side and girls on the other. There was little interaction between the sexes—at least not when white supervisors were watching. They were formally instructed in English, which they learned by rote. What they enjoyed most in school was to sing. It was easier to learn English by singing than by speaking.

The girls all looked the same in chin-length bobs. They wore gray-wool ankle-length dresses with long sleeves and high, tight collars. They were clumsy in stiff high-topped shoes. Their discarded clothes, blankets, and shorn braids were burned in the yard—except for the quilled or beaded moccasins and leggings. The school's staff kept all these prime examples of Indian artifacts. Some they sold to collectors or, fortunately, to museums.

One teacher recalled that reservation boarding schools were isolated institutions that were self-sustaining, with the children doing the work. In a "sewing room, with its rows of pedaled machines, the older girls made all the clothing worn by two hundred pupils, with the exception of the boys' Sunday uniforms," the teacher remembered. "Cotton work dresses and shirts, gingham and flannel uniforms for the girls, work aprons, petticoats, night-

Students hanging up
laundry at Pine Ridge
Day School No. 29.
*South Dakota State
Historical Society*

Saint Mary's Mission
School girls' choir,
Rosebud Indian
Reservation. *South
Dakota State Historical
Society*

gowns, tablecloths, sheets, and towels in endless number." The
girls also mended clothes and darned stockings, did the laundry,
ironed, and scrubbed the floors.[5]

Indian agencies and school facilities resembled United States
military forts. After the morning chores were done and before
classes, all students assembled in the open square of the school
campus. My grandmothers and mother recalled the drills they
had to learn. They stood in straight lines according to their age
group, boys on one side and girls on the other, with the youngest
children in the front rows. They marched in step, swinging their
arms in unison; they turned their heads toward the teachers who
reviewed their movements. They all halted in front of the flag-
pole, where they solemnly watched the red, white, and blue ban-
ner rise above their heads. I cringe at the irony of the ceremony,
which trained American Indians to be patriots before they were
legal citizens of the United States.

Sewing room, boarding school, Pine Ridge Indian Reservation. *South Dakota State Historical Society*

In the first month of school, older boys formed a brass band. My mother had wanted to be in the band, but only boys were allowed. However, she recalled how fun it became to step in time to military marches. My father and other boys wore smart uniforms that attracted feminine admiration. After the daily drill, the boys and girls marched to the classroom for morning academic classes; industrial training was in the afternoon. Then, those who did not have to prepare supper had free time outdoors.

"Oh, we loved the outdoor time," my grandmother recalled. Even when fall breezes gave way to cold winds with stings of snow, the children burst from the stifling closeness of the school walls. Still separated by gender, groups of girls ran around the square; the rushing wind gave an illusion of freedom. They walked in the strongest gales; the white adults sought shelter, but they could

Sewing room, Lower Cut Meat School, 1897.
National Anthropological Archives, Smithsonian Institution

Girls playing outside
Pierre Indian School.
*South Dakota State
Historical Society*

not contain their pupils. Outdoors, they were not the docile students, and they passively ignored commands to "Come in!"

On Saturdays, there were no classes, but the children had to bathe. The little girls bathed in their dormitory and changed into clean clothing. Then they ate while the older girls bathed. Next was religious instruction held in the classrooms. The students, boys on one side and girls on the other, sat quietly listening to a Christian minister from the agency until he stopped talking, then they rushed outdoors. Those students who had brothers and sisters spent the time together. The little ones tightly grasped an older sibling's hand to walk or huddle out of the wind. Sometimes

Sioux school girls playing with toy tipis, Pine Ridge Indian Reservation, 1891.
South Dakota State Historical Society

unrelated boys and girls managed time together before they separated for the evening meal.

Sunday, after breakfast and morning chores, the student body and teachers stood in line to go to church. The smallest were in front, the older students in the rear, with dormitory staff and teachers separating the boys and girls. They marched to the agency church for services. Some Christian denominations had exclusive presence on particular reservations. During President Ulysses Grant's administration, military supervision on the reservations ended, and Christian churches were given oversight. In South Dakota, the Yankton, Crow Creek, Cheyenne River, Pine Ridge, and Rosebud reservations were Episcopal. Standing Rock was Roman Catholic; Sisseton and Flandreau were Presbyterian.[6] Episcopal and Presbyterian missionaries allowed the use of native languages in prayer books and hymnals.

My grandmother recalled that the children did not balk at attending church because they could hear and speak Dakota. When the minister spoke, bright eyes watched, and ears avidly listened to their native tongue. Not a single young child fidgeted. This quiet attentiveness was the proper attitude for youth when a respected elder spoke. More so, the Dakota phrases were comforting to hear, even if the listeners did not comprehend the message.

"Oh, how we enjoyed the hymns, and we sang loud," Grandma smiled. She did not say so, but part of the reason they joined in was because, as I noted earlier, it was easier to sing the English words than to speak them.

After the service, the children marched back to school. "The Sunday dinner was good," Grandma remembered. "We had potatoes or rice in gravy and two dried apricots or prunes as a treat." Those first children at boarding schools often had bleeding gums, and their teeth would loosen and fall out. My grandmothers just said they got sick from the food, but it must have been scurvy from the lack of Vitamin C in their diet. The children loved the dried fruit added to the meals.

(*opposite*)
Meal servers, Pine Ridge boarding school, 1900. *South Dakota State Historical Society*

Grandma Flora recalled that Sunday afternoon was the best part of the week. "We had free time outdoors, and we walked close together in the hard wind over the parade ground until we had to go in. It was too cold. Our teeth chattered." In the shelter of a building, they lingered in the gathering darkness. "We heard the geese and looked up to see them fly in a 'v' in the sky. They sounded sad, and I wanted to fly with them—to home."

The cold reminded Grandma of how it had been at home on a frigid day in a cold log house. The family lay on a worn buffalo robe huddled on wool army blankets. The adults took turns dashing to the small iron stove, tossing in logs, then back to the bed. She told me: "Unci, Grandma, gave us a pinch of wasna [dried chokecherries/suet trail food]; the grownups had melted snow. Unci filled her iron kettle with snow, added a few strips of dried meat, a handful of tipsila [wild turnips] into a broth that simmered all day. Finally, in the dark evening, after the wind ceased and the cabin still warm from the stove's heat, Unci gave us each a cup of soup." Grandma Flora's eyes misted as she remembered those times. At school, the children hoped those at home now had more to eat. The agent had threatened to stop the family's rations if the children did not go to school.

As preparations for Christmas began in the Moon When Horns Are Broken Off, the time the whites call the month of December, Grandma wondered what made Christmas special. The following story is based on my grandmother's recollections and the experiences of the Reverend Andrew Weston, Episcopal priest, as told later in a Christmas sermon in Flandreau, South Dakota.[7]

The students were uneasy and restless. The teachers in the classroom and in the dorms, the cooks in the kitchen, the janitors, and the dairyman were talking about Christmas and wondering how it was going to be out here in this God forsaken country. The girls, who worked in the kitchen, reported that they had been set to work making thirty-eight pumpkin pies with sugar, and they had used most of the milk so that there was none for breakfast. This fact did not distress the children, for they intensely disliked milk. The pies were for Christmas dinner.

The big boys who worked in the dairy and helped shovel snow had unloaded barrels of apples from the freight wagon. The fruit would be the children's Christmas gift. All the talk of Christmas, the anticipated treat of pumpkin pie with sugar and no molasses, and the apples they all loved indicated to Grandma Flora that Christmas was a day more special than any other. Then, why was Christmas to start at night with a service in the agency chapel?

The students quietly marched from the school to the chapel. Snow crunched beneath their hard-soled shoes, which they still hated even though their first blisters had healed. It was odd to be going to church in the dark; some of the bigger boys had spoken of slipping away in the night, but the bright starlight would give them away. So they followed the little students and girls to the church.

Amber streams of light flowed from the windows of the small frame building, and the march quickened toward the beckoning warmth. As the first student stepped onto the porch, the door opened and the minister, Mr. Burt, in his white robe, helped the little ones into the church. Eyes blinked in the yellow glow of kerosene lamps hanging from the ceiling, the oily smoke sharp in cold nostrils. The smallest boys and girls walked to the front with their teacher; the girls filed in behind, and then the men and boys sat on the other side with the biggest in the rear near the pot-bellied stove. It was the warmest place in the church but not the most comfortable, for it was soon too hot. However, it was their duty to keep the fire going during the service.

Not a child uttered a word, but bright eyes gazed at the transformation of the plain sanctuary. Swags of green cedar boughs hung over each window, above the altar, and on the organ where Mrs. Burt sat. She smiled a welcome at the little ones as her feet

Food preparation, Flandreau Indian School.
South Dakota State Historical Society

pumped the organ into wheezing bellows and played a carol the students had practiced.

They stood, as they had been trained, and sang. They knelt and listened to prayers in Dakota. Next, they sat as the minister stood beside the lectern and told the Christmas story. The birth of a baby was common to the children; it was a natural event in their homes, but the idea of the baby's parents being turned away from lodging was foreign to a people who were always welcomed in any village. The minister spoke of wise men coming to see the baby, which students also understood. A birth of a baby was a joyous time, and the elders, wise men of the band, would especially welcome the birth because it meant the survival of the tribe.

The door creaked open, and a draft of cold darted over their ankles, but none of the well-trained children turned until they heard the soft shuffle of moccasins. Now heads turned, but the children showed no excitement as young eyes followed three Indian men moving up the aisle. The first was the aged chief Drifting Goose, still starkly erect for his years, leading two other elders; all wore blankets draped over their shoulders. Behind them, their blanket-wrapped women aligned themselves near the stove.

Mr. Burt stopped speaking as the chief neared the lectern. He stepped forward as the men came to him, and they shook hands. The teacher of the little ones nervously fluttered up from the front pew, pulling children off on the floor, but Drifting Goose held up his hand and shook his head; he and his men sat at Mr. Burt's feet. The story resumed.

The minister spoke of shepherds watching their sheep in the cold night. Shepherds and sheep? The children silently wondered what they were, and what was an angel? Was this a story of a vision quest when young men went out alone to seek a spirit helper?

The sermon ended. Readily, the children rose and sang "O Little Town of Bethlehem," which they had practiced and memorized without grasping its meaning. Now the words and the meaning came together in their minds, and they understood that the hymn was the story the minister had just told.

Seated again, the students watched Mr. Burt prepare the bread and wine at the altar and wondered why their teachers knelt so humbly at the rail, eating the bread and sipping the wine. They quietly marveled that Drifting Goose and his party also knelt at the communion rail. If a chief converted, often his whole band would too.

"Mmmmooo," quietly sounded from outdoors, causing the boys by the windows to stare into the dark night.

"Moooo," louder.

Then the bass of men's voices rumbled over creaking leather, and again a dart of cold air swirled as the door creaked open. This time feet stomped and spurs jangled as two booted cowboys came into the church. They took off their hats, nodded to Mr. Burt, and opened their long canvass mackinaws to the warmth of the stove. None of the children stirred, but they knew of these white men who trailed cattle to their reservation homes—maybe to theirs.

Again, the organ wheezed as Mrs. Burt pumped and began the final carol. The cowboys pulled out their sacks of tobacco and papers and rolled a smoke as the children sang, "o come all ye faithful."

Drifting Goose and his elders stood. From under his blanket, the chief pulled his pipe bag and walked to the stove. He tamped knikinic (willow bark) into the red stone bowl, and one of the cowboys struck a match. The old chief drew on the pipe and offered it to the sky, the earth, and each direction before he smoked and shared the pipe with his men and the cowboys.

The singing stopped; the cowboys, warm and rested, left the church, raising a hand in thanks to Mr. Burt. Leather creaked as they mounted their horses and followed the herd. Drifting Goose wrapped his blanket securely about his tall form, lifted a hand sign of peace and farewell to Mr. Burt, and led his men and women into the night.

Flora and Robert Driving Hawk with son James Driving Hawk (on horse), 1925.
Virginia Driving Hawk Sneve Collection

The big boys carried sleeping little ones and led the way back to the school. Bright stars lit their way; snow crunched underfoot; cows mooed in the distance; and the deep voice of an Indian man commanded the horses that pulled the wagon that carried Drifting Goose to his home near the river. The harness bells jingled away to silence.

Grandma sat quietly gazing out of the window as she ended her recollections. "It was a good time," she mused. "Even though I missed being home, I learned a lot—how to cook, wash clothes, clean house, and I learned to read, write, and to do arithmetic. All that helped me get along in the white world. I made friends that I had all my life. And I met Robert." She smiled and wiped a tear, "So it was a good time."

Before there were day schools on the reservation, Sioux children went to boarding schools, as we have seen. Some schools, run with military correctness, were located far away in the East: Carlisle Indian School in Pennsylvania and Hampton Institute in Virginia. Others, such as White's Manual Institute in Indiana, were run by religious denominations. In the 1880s and 1890s, the Roman Catholic, Episcopal, and Presbyterian churches opened boarding schools closer to home on Sioux reservations. No matter which institution a young woman attended, the experience had lasting effects on her life. Some saw the schools as destroying cultural identity, but others viewed them as having provided opportunities that allowed them to succeed in the dominant society.

The Holy Rosary Mission (now Red Cloud Indian School) on the Pine Ridge reservation and Saint Francis on the Rosebud were Catholic institutions. Priests and nuns operated the schools with strict supervision, some being harsher than others. Delphine Red Shirt told of her mother's experience at Red Cloud: "Mom-mah had boarded there as a young girl. She hated it. She said she admired the older girls who grew proficient at throwing large buns at the nuns when they turned their backs. They were given freshly baked buns for a snack, and many of the older girls kept theirs until they hardened. Then they used them as missiles, which they launched and fired at nuns they didn't like. . . . [B]y the time the nuns turned around in their heavy habits, the girl hurling the bun was standing silent and still. She said the hardest thing about her experience there was kneeling so long at mass."[1]

Today, we are aware of sexual abuse of boys by priests in Catholic schools,[2] but we rarely hear of nuns abusing girls. Friends of mine who attended Saint Francis told of nuns having girls

Classroom,
Carlisle Indian School,
Pennsylvania. *Cumberland
County Historical Society*

Saint Mary's Mission School, Rosebud Indian Reservation. *South Dakota State Historical Society*

hold towels for bathing nuns, of nuns fondling their breasts or watching girls in the shower. However, more often, it was verbal and physical abuse; nuns shouted, slapped, or hit with rulers. The students told their parents, who refused to believe that holy women acted that way. Still, some girls did not experience abuse and were devout converts. Marie Therese Archambault, Oglala Sioux, graduated from Saint Francis, went on to study scriptures, and earned a master's degree in theology. She taught in mission schools for twenty years and eventually lived in Rome.[3]

The Episcopal schools had lay administrators and teachers, and they often employed local Indians as janitors, cooks, and dormitory aids. These schools required a nominal tuition payment. If parents could not pay, they brought fresh produce from their home gardens. The schools also had large vegetable gardens, where the students learned to plant, harvest, and preserve. Other sources of tuition were the women's societies in the students' home communities.

William McK. Chapman spent three years running Saint Elizabeth's School for Indian Boys and Girls on the Standing Rock reservation. He wrote his memoir of that time in which he admitted to receiving "an education in prairie life and Indian ways."[4] The stoic, uncommunicative students baffled him, and he soon learned where their loyalty lay. When some of the bigger girls sneaked out of the dorms, a little girl told on them, but she gave no names. Chapman called a school assembly, hoping to find out the identity of the culprits. "I made a rather pompous speech about law and order," he said, "and that one of the purposes of St. Elizabeth's was to protect its girls from some of the rougher aspects of the world, which it certainly could not do if the girls went out of the windows at night. . . . I urged Ted and Joe [reservation police] to whip out their fingerprinting kit and do their stuff. There was no response of any kind from any one."[5] None of the students or Indian staff would identify the girls; their loyalty was to each other, not to him.

My grandmother Flora Driving Hawk, three aunts, and I attended Saint Mary's Episcopal School for girls. Flora attended the school when it was in Mission, South Dakota, on the Rosebud reservation. She stayed until she finished the equivalent of the fifth grade. (She later attended a boarding school in Chamberlain on the Missouri River, where she met Robert Driving Hawk.) Besides academic work, Flora learned basic domestic and academic skills. Many of the girls learned to play the organ so that they could be organists in their home churches. The girls of Saint Mary's were proud of their training and so was Bishop William H. Hare (founder of the school), who reported, "One can pick out a St. Mary's girl wherever she goes in the Indian country by the kind of home she keeps."[6]

When I attended in the 1950s, I received much the same education that Flora had, but the emphasis was on high-school academics and social skills to benefit the girls in college. However, there were still incidents of "sneaking out at night." The old build-

ing had hollow-tube fire escapes, and several of us big girls slid down and into the night. As I recall, we ran about the campus, giggled for a while, and then got cold. When we crawled up the tubes to get into the dorms, the top entrance was blocked. Back down we went and found teachers guiding us through the front door. We forgot that the tubes resounded loudly when so many slid down, and the staff knew that we had gone out.

From the earliest years, many of the male and female students who attended these boarding schools wed after they returned to the reservation, and these unions led to acculturated families adapting traditional habits to the "civilized," or white, lifestyles they had learned at school. The young people had often converted to Christianity and became active leaders in local congregations; women took part in prayer meetings and *winyan omniciye*, the women's societies organized by the missionaries.

They learned how to bead, to make moccasins, and to do other traditional craftwork that they sold. They used the money for local projects or to support native missionaries now ministering to their own people.[7]

Early missionary Mary Riggs, who worked with the Sioux in Minnesota and Nebraska, described some of the women's work: "The women were skilful in cutting designs of flowers, birds and butterflies from bright colored calicos, and hemming them daintily onto unbleached muslin for table covers and quilts. They were very fond of patchwork, and even crazy patchwork soon found its way into the homes of the Indian women."[8] Thus, in the nineteenth century, Sioux women learned to make quilts, a craft that would become an art form in the twentieth century. The western Sioux preferred the star quilt because it resembled the traditional geometric quill design of the morning star, a symbol of a new day and life.[9]

Before reservation settlement, women of one family had helped another tan hides or prepare a lodge cover, all the while gossiping, laughing, or weeping—sharing community sorrow and joy. Therefore, the gathering of *winyan omniciye* kept this tradition alive. On the reservation, women no longer lived in the shelter and closeness of a tipi in the camp circle but in log cabins and rough-hewn houses. Reservation teacher Elaine Goodale Eastman described how boarding-school education made a difference in such dwellings. "A typical Indian cabin of the poorer sort," she wrote, "will be made a hundred times more attractive within by the deft fingers of the little daughter who has learned to wash dishes, sweep, and make neat beds at the school."[10] Such cleaning had not been necessary in a tipi, where women rolled up the bottoms to let fresh air circulate, aired out buffalo robes, and cleaned the fire pit. They moved the tipi when the site was soiled. A log cabin did not move, and its confining closeness was ideal for breeding disease. Now, former boarding school girls kept such houses clean.

A tipi with its edge rolled up for ventilation. *South Dakota State Historical Society*

Later, the Bureau of Indian Affairs established day schools to provide elementary education nearer to family homes. Small children no longer had to go away to school. Boarding-school educated women and mothers encouraged their children to attend and learn.

One of these early educated Sioux women was Zitkala-sa (Red Bird), whose English name was Gertrude Bonnin after she married Ray Bonnin, a Sioux man. She was born on the Yankton reservation but left to attend White's Manual Institute, a Quaker boarding school in Wabash, Indiana. Three years later, she returned to the reservation, where she found herself torn, as she said, "neither a wild Indian, nor a tame one."[11]

She returned to the white world, went to Earlham College in Richmond, Indiana, and became a teacher. She was not an outgoing student, was shy among others, but she won oratory contests. She published *Old Indian Legends* (1901), a collection of Sioux stories, and became an activist for American Indian causes. She taught at the Carlisle Indian School and began writing essays for *The Atlantic Monthly* and *Harper's* magazines. According to one biographer: "Zitkala-Sa began publicly to express her estrangement from both cultures and her indignation over the treatment of her people by state and church. She articulated her struggle with cultural dislocation and injustice and thereby became an earnest bridge builder between cultures, using language as a tool to forge an identity encompassing both cultures." Zitkala-Sa was a proponent of the Indian Citizenship Bill in 1924 and, after all adult Indians were given the vote, persuaded them to vote for Franklin Roosevelt.[12]

Another educated Sioux woman who used her education to further the culture of her people was Ella Deloria, born in 1889. She was the daughter of Reverend Philip Deloria and aunt to the well-known activist and author Vine Deloria. She attended All Saints School in Sioux Falls and college at Oberlin, Ohio, and Columbia University in New York. She worked with anthropologist Franz Boas and researched and studied Indian languages and culture, publishing *Dakota Texts* in 1932, *Dakota Grammar* in 1942, and *Speaking of Indians* in 1944, as well as several short articles. In her novel *Waterlily* (1988), she told of a Sioux girl growing to womanhood in the era just before white settlers changed that life forever. Throughout her life, Ella Deloria valued and kept her connection to family and community in South Dakota.[13]

Agnes Ross, who was born in 1910 near Flandreau, South Dakota, and educated to be a teacher, had an unusual experience for a young Sioux woman of the twentieth century. In 1938, she was named a representative to the conference of Christian youth in Amsterdam, Holland. After the conference, the United States

(opposite)
Zitkala-Sa, also known as Gertrude Bonnin.
National Portrait Gallery, Smithsonian Institution

Agnes and
Harvey Ross,
the author's
aunt and
uncle, on their
fiftieth wedding
anniversary.
*Virginia Driving
Hawk Sneve
Collection*

government sent her to Denmark to a workshop on how to form cooperatives. She traveled by train from Brussels with two Norwegian girls, and before they changed trains in Berlin, they toured the city. Soldiers with Nazi armbands stopped her and tore up her tickets because they thought she was a Jew. The Norwegian girls ran to the American consulate, which arranged for her tickets to be replaced."[14]

Agnes, whose Indian name was Wihopa (Beautiful Woman), made it safely home to finish college, teach on South Dakota reservations, marry Harvey Ross, and bear four sons. She was also the keeper of the Santee Sioux women's medicine bundle, which was used for female power. She inherited it from her Great-grandmother Standing Cloud. She was also the first woman to be chairperson of the Flandreau Sioux tribe.[15]

A contemporary of Agnes's was Evelyn Lambert Bergen, a Yankton Sioux born in 1907. She boarded at All Saints School in Sioux Falls, South Dakota, a private girls' school with few Indian students. She received her B.S. from Carleton College in Northfield, Minnesota. She taught in Bureau of Indian Affairs and public schools in South Dakota for over forty years. She also served on the South Dakota State Board of Education.[16] She and Agnes Ross encouraged many students to go on to higher education, and they both encouraged me in my writing career.

While many of the girls who went to boarding schools wed classmates on the reservation, others married descendants of French traders and Sioux women. As a result, the surnames LeBeau, Clairmont, Lapointe, Antoine, Dupree, Laframbois, to name a few, are prevalent on Sioux reservations. Others wed Anglo-Saxon descendants of traders and military men: Ross, McKenzie, Jackson, Raymond, and Conroy are some examples. Mexican descent can be found in names such as Giago, Hernandez, and Gallego. Many of these couples became ranchers, taking to the life with horses and working cattle as their nomad ancestors had pursued buffalo. Still other girls found mates among the full-blooded men such

President Calvin Coolidge, his wife, and Rosebud Yellow Robe, 1928. *South Dakota State Historical Society*

as Driving Hawk, Iron Shell, Two Bulls, Two Hawk, and Standing Bear. Some of these men also married white women. Chauncey Yellow Robe, an example of a full-blooded man who married a white woman, had three daughters, Rosebud, Chauncina, and Evelyn.

Rosebud Yellow Robe, born in Rapid City in 1907, went to the University of South Dakota, where she gained attention for her program of Indian dances. In 1927, she and her father presented President Calvin Coolidge with a Lakota headdress on his visit to the Black Hills. After she married and moved to New York City, Rosebud began working at Jones Beach State Park in 1930. Before long, she was directing the Jones Beach Indian Village, where she shared Indian culture with local children by telling legends, singing songs, and teaching handcrafts. Rosebud's performances followed the more spectacular Buffalo Bill Cody's Wild West shows (1883–1917), and like Cody, she capitalized on the non-Indian's fascination with American Indians. She appeared on national radio and television and authored *Album of the American Indian* (1969) and *Tonweya and the Eagles* (1979), which was translated into various international languages.[17]

Rosebud's sister Chauncina Yellow Robe worked for the R. H. Donnelly Corporation in advertising and sales after she left South Dakota. She married an Arapaho, Lee White Horse, and both were active in national Indian affairs. Chauncina led the Native American Committee of Chicago and received a McNickle Fellowship from the Newberry Library to research the historical treatment of American Indian elderly. Evelyn Yellow Robe, who grew up in New York, had less connection to her Indian heritage. She majored in speech pathology and eventually moved to Germany.[18]

Many Sioux girls stayed on the reservation, where they also adapted to white culture. "The 1920s produced hosts of reservation flappers," anthropologist Marla Powers noted, "complete with cloche hats fitted rakishly over bobbed hair, short skirts, dark stockings, and ankle-strap shoes (much to the chagrin of the grandmothers, who continued to wear their long calico dresses and deerskin moccasins). . . . The 1930s were an extension of the twenties with somewhat longer skirts." In the 1940s, the reservation girls continued to dress much like the rest of the United States.[19] In my era of the fifties, we wore rolled-up jeans, boys' white shirts, and bobby socks. My grandmothers still preferred long dresses, kerchiefs tied about their heads, and feet shod in black-leather laced shoes with a chunky heel—"gramma shoes."

Many of these grandmothers continued to teach daughters and granddaughters traditional skills that also served them in their new lives. My grandmothers made a few dollars by selling their creations, and my mother, who followed her mother in making dolls, sold them to collectors in California. She thought twenty dollars was a lot to get for one of her creations, but thirty years later, she found her dolls in an antique shop priced at one hundred fifty dollars each. Elsie Flood, who did beadwork in the 1950s, said, "It pays me better than going out and cleaning house

Bobbed hair and 1950s fashions at
Wahpeton Indian School, North Dakota.
South Dakota State Historical Society

or washing for people."[20] Another craftswoman was Zelda Gallegos, who marketed her Indian dolls at craft shows; today, her
work is represented in art galleries and private collections. Alice
Blue Legs, an Oglala, was a skilled quillwork artist who sold to
collectors all over the world. Other modern Sioux women such as
Joanne Bird have careers in visual arts, and her daughter, Jackie,
is a musician and hoop dancer. Both Joanne and Jackie were students at the Flandreau Indian boarding school.[21]

During World War II, some women wore military uniforms
when they joined the large numbers of reservation men who enlisted in the armed services. My aunt Olive Ross of Rosebud was
a Women's Army Corps member. Rose Ashley of Rosebud joined
the United States Navy, and Marcella LeBeau of Cheyenne River
served in the United States Army Nurse Corps. There were also
Sioux women in the service during the Korean Conflict and the
Vietnam War. In 2011, Crow Creek tribal member Major Stephanie
R. Griffith, United States Marine Corps, was awarded the Bronze
Star for meritorious service to her country in Afghanistan. To-

Marcella LeBeau (left) and her friend Bette Rohay on duty in Europe during World War II. *Rapid City Journal*

Major Stephanie R. Griffith (left) during her service in Afghanistan with the United States Marine Corps. *Native Sun News*

day, more women have also joined in what were once only male rituals, such as a vision quest and the sun dance. I have female cousins who danced at the latter, and our aunt, Agnes Ross, was honored as the grandmother for the Black Hills sun dance.[22]

No matter how they dress or what they do, modern Sioux women do not shy from controversy. For example, the Oglala Sioux Tribe's first female president, Cecilia Fire Thunder, challenged the state of South Dakota's law banning abortions. A nurse, Cecilia defied the law and, citing the reservation's sovereignty, made plans to establish a family-planning clinic on tribal land. The male tribal council impeached her for acting without their approval. A young college student, Serena Clifford, attended the impeachment hearing. "I looked up to her [Fire Thunder]," said

Clifford. "I couldn't understand why she wasn't being allowed to help women make their own choices."[23] The documentary film *Young Lakota* shows the resulting political fallout and Clifford's reaction.

Author Elizabeth Cook-Lynn, born on the Crow Creek reservation, became a university professor and one of the founding editors of *Wicazo Sa Review,* an academic journal for American Indian studies. She published *The Politics of Hallowed Ground: Wounded Knee and the Struggle for Indian Sovereignty* (with Mario Gonzalez, 1998) and *Why I Can't Read Wallace Stegner and Other Essays: A Tribal Voice* (1991). Cook-Lynn has been an active voice in Rapid City community affairs, speaking at city council meetings to support a sculpture garden of contemporary Indian leaders and urging the passage of an ordinance against racial discrimination.[24] Contemporary Sioux women can thus be activists, and there is much for them to be concerned about. On November 13, 2013, the *Rapid City Journal* printed an Associated Press release about the findings of a national panel of judicial and law-enforcement experts. These people had surveyed safety concerns on reservations, where the violent crime rate is up to twenty times the national average. Dozens of American Indian women are raped each day across the United States. Part of the panel's recommendations was to give tribes more control over crime and justice on their reservations.[25] Another important piece of the recommendation was to enforce the provisions of the Violence against Women Act of 1994, designed to "combat violence against Indian women and children and develop and strengthen victim services particularly involving violent crimes against women."[26] Marla Powers's 1986 study of the Oglala tribe had noted that Pine Ridge "has not escaped a concern of national import: the abusive treatment of women."[27]

What had happened to a society that respected women and believed that striking in anger damaged both the victim and the perpetrator's spirit? Mothers and daughters had been respected and cherished in prereservation times, when men sat in council but women influenced their decisions. In the past, even when I was a teen on the reservation, a woman whose husband beat her could still find safety in her family. She and her children were welcomed at home. Brothers and uncles pursued and reprimanded the abuser. A wife could still divorce a husband by putting his belongings outside her door, and if she proceeded to a legal divorce, her family supported her financially.

Much of that has changed. One Oglala woman explained it in this way. After World War II, men began to beat their wives: "They learned it in the army when they were able to go out drinking and socializing with non-Indians. They saw a life different from the one they lived on the reservation. When they came home, they were so frustrated that there were no opportunities available, they just lashed out at their wives."[28]

Incidents of abuse can be found on all South Dakota reservations, and they are directly related to alcohol use by both men and women. During the fur-trade years, alcohol had been introduced to Indian men, and female status had deteriorated as husbands began bartering the pelts their wives had tanned for guns and whiskey. Later, the Indian relatives of women married to traders became so dependent on trade goods and whiskey that they no longer hunted to supply food or shelter. As Indian men became addicted to alcohol, fathers, brothers, and husbands traded their daughters, sisters, and wives for whiskey. It became even more disastrous when Indian women became addicted to alcohol as well and prostituted themselves to obtain it.

In modern times, some Indians still engage in binge drinking. It was the way their great grandparents had learned to drink. It reflected how nomadic tribes consumed food. When there was plenty, one ate it all, for no one knew when there would be another full plate. Women who drank while pregnant began to bear children afflicted with fetal alcohol syndrome. An effect of the syndrome is that these children have poor reasoning and judg-

Winyan omniciye, or women's guild, in Okreek, South Dakota. *Virginia Driving Hawk Sneve Collection*

ment skills.[29] Alcohol and drugs on the reservation and in urban areas led to battering, especially of women. Today, if a woman flees the violence, she often leaves with only the clothes on her back.

All of these things have been a catastrophe for Indian cultures, but Sioux women have begun to adapt to this tragedy in various ways. As their daughters and granddaughters move into income-producing jobs away from home, grandmothers are often the steadying center of families. They delight in their grandchildren even though they may not understand the world in which they live. Sometimes, grandchildren come to the grandmothers' homes for safe shelter after their own mothers have fled abusive husbands or boyfriends. Sioux women have also worked within the community to find safe places for women and children who lack family support. In 1977, the White Buffalo Calf Woman Society women's shelter opened on the Rosebud reservation. In 2013, it provided shelter and services to 176 victims.[30] Since then, other reservations have started similar programs, and some can be found in towns bordering reservations and serving both Indians and non-Indians.

Sioux grandmothers also continue to teach their grandchildren that past values have a place in the modern world and that the White Buffalo Calf Woman's instructions are still important. My grandmother Flora Driving Hawk lived with us, and she looked forward to the end of the school day when my children came home. She told them stories that she had related to me as a child. Sometimes she would forget an aspect of the tale and say to me, "You tell it," and as I did, she would correct my version as she remembered hers. She had once done intricate beadwork with thin needles with miniscule eyes and had quilted until her eyesight dimmed and arthritis crippled her fingers. She taught me to quilt, saying, "So you can make quilts for your grandchildren."

Few Indian boarding schools are left in the nation today, and the women who attended them continue to have mixed feelings about the education they received. Sometimes the schools contributed to cultural destruction, but in other cases, women used the education to seize opportunities that allowed them to succeed in the dominant culture while remaining rooted in Sioux tradition.

ndian students now go to public schools, but they stay in dormitories if they live beyond bus transportation. Public and private religious high schools are located in the major communities on reservations such as Pine Ridge and Rosebud. Girls still meet boys at school sporting events, dances, movies, powwows, or at a sun dance. Marla Powers noted, "A long-standing joke has it that children are born nine months after the Sun Dance. This may not be so much of a joke since in the past it was at the large annual meetings that non-kin had the opportunity to meet and develop friendships and intimacy."[1] Today, a powwow, or *wacipi,* the gathering's traditional name, meaning "place where they danced," is a colorful event drawing male and female competitors from all parts of the reservation or, for the larger ones like the Black Hills Powwow, from all parts of North and South America. The powwow has come to represent American Indian culture because it is so highly visible.

The males are the most vibrant participants in feathered bustles, porcupine hairpieces, beaded armbands, cuffs, belts, and moccasins. They dance assertively, stomping, bending, bobbing, and weaving in intricate steps. Women wear what have been termed "traditional" beaded buckskin or cloth dresses adorned with elk teeth, dentalium, or cowrie shells, beaded leggings, and moccasins. They carry an eagle-wing fan and/or a fringed shawl over their arm. They move in short sedate steps to the beat of the drum. Sometimes, a woman stands close to a male drum group to sing with the men and "trill" her approval of the songs.

At smaller reservation powwows, girls dance more freely, not worrying about competition. Delphine Red Shirt described her experience: "We flung long cloth shawls upon our backs, over T-shirts and jeans. These shawls are called 'šina kaswpi,' 'šina'

A dance near the Grand River
before 1918. *South Dakota State
Historical Society*

meaning 'shawl' and 'kaswpi' referring to the long 'fringes' decorating the cloth shawl. . . . I wore moccasins, and my feet felt light upon the grass where the wacipi were held. I listened to the drummers so sure in their song. . . . I watched how the old women danced, swinging their śinas back and forth rhythmically. . . . The announcer at the powwow called out, 'Hokahe, hokahe, wacipi yo, wacipi yo, wacipi yo,' which means, 'Strengthen your hearts, be strong, dance, dance, dance.'"[2]

At the competitive powwows, some younger women dance similarly to the men in the shawl dance. They hold their shawls in outspread arms so that the shawl frills swing wildly in time to the drum. There are also women who dance in bright satin fabric trimmed with gleaming rows of shiny cones, a jingle dress. The origin of the dress began "when a father was worried about his daughter who was ill. One night, he dreamed that he rolled tobacco-can lids into cones, and his mother sewed them on a dress for the little girl. He remembered the dream after he woke and knew that his dead mother, the little girl's grandmother, had sent him a message. He gathered hundreds of lids from men of the tribe to make the cones. The girl's mother sewed them on a special dress. The little girl put on the dress, and as she danced, she grew strong. The illness left her, and she was well.[3] Today, the jingle dance is a separate category of dance types at powwows; the dancers should be pure young women and girls.

Grandmothers often encourage their children to dance. In a story about children learning to dance, a *Rapid City Journal* reporter talked to Delores Hayes, a grandmother from Standing Rock reservation. Hayes said that dancing is one of the most positive things in the lives of children, grandchildren, and great-grandchildren. "It gives you a good feeling," she said. "If you feel bad, you just dance and all your problems go away."[4]

Powwows are also stages for honoring and connecting with larger community than the immediate family. At some powwows, giveaways may be held in the name of someone who has accom-

Delphine Red Shirt, 1999. *Native Sun News*

plished many things and now must honor those who helped him/ her reach his/her goal. In non-Indian society, such an individual is honored with a gold watch or, the most esteemed honor, a Nobel prize. In American Indian society, the family gives gifts in the honoree's name to persons important in his/her life.

The family prepares months or years for the giveaway. Grandmothers, aunts, and female relatives make star quilts, the most valued item. They require the most expense, not only in purchase of the fabric, but also in time needed to make them. The most important person will receive a quilt, but all others in attendance will receive a gift, such as purchased blankets, clothing, combs, or mirrors; toys and candy will go to the children.

Woman dancing
the jingle dance at a
powwow, 2005.
*National Museum of
the American Indian,
Smithsonian Institution*

Danielle TaSheena Finn, Standing Rock Sioux Tribe, crowned Miss Indian World 2016. *The Gathering of Nations*

The author's granddaughter, Bonita Rickers, wearing her jingle dress. *Virginia Driving Hawk Sneve Collection*

The giveaway is ceremonial and reminds the honoree that he/she is not alone in life. Community, *tiyospaye*, will support the individual in hard times and will acknowledge achievement now or after death. At these public honoring ceremonies, most often held at powwows, special songs are sung in honor or memory of the individual. All attending will enter the honoree's circle to shake hands with him/her and all the family. The people move in time to the drum beat, shake hands or embrace, moving in the sacred circle.

Today, there are powwow queens and princesses who wear Miss America-style sashes across their bodies noting the reservations they represent, such as Miss Rosebud or Junior Miss Cheyenne River. They will follow the military honor guard made up of current members or veterans of past conflicts who lead the procession of the powwow's grand entry—the most vividly colored part of the event. It is a sensory occasion that heightens emotions. As in the past, such events sometimes lead to the conception of babies. The girl's parents are often upset, but when the baby arrives, it is welcomed and loved.

Single mothers may raise children on federal assistance subsidies. If a young mother can find a job, her own mother will be the child's caregiver. If the grandmother also works outside of the home, the great-grandmother cares for the children. Often the child's sire is not part of the home, but a grandfather sometimes will fulfill that role. Powers described this situation in the 1980s, but it is still true in the twenty-first century. One of the women she interviewed told her: "I think that women are taking a more responsible position as far as family life is concerned. As far as thinking we have to get ahead, we do because we have to feed our families. While the men are just sitting back and saying 'Man, this is bad and there's nothing we can do about it,' women feel that they have a responsibility to the family. *She* has to take care of the kids."[5]

Women had begun to take responsibility as early as the 1930s,

A Brule mother and
her children, ca. 1950.
*South Dakota State
Historical Society*

when they traveled with their families from reservations to summer jobs picking potatoes or other migrant labor. Older children
helped pick or minded younger children as their mothers toiled
beside their husbands. During the years of World War II, Indian
women and men worked at the Black Hills Army Ordinance De-
pot in Igloo, near Edgemont, South Dakota. Others found employment at military installations in Rapid City and Sioux Falls.

After the war, Indians who returned to the reservation did not
resume life in isolated reservation communities based on subsis-

tence farming. The few employment opportunities available on the reservations paid extremely low wages. Many families moved to towns bordering reservations such as Winner, Gregory, Wagner, and Sisseton or to South Dakota's two largest cities—Rapid City and Sioux Falls—to find employment. Women also moved with their families to Sioux Falls to be near husbands or sons who served sentences in the state penitentiary. Change came as families moved away from the closeness of *tiyospaye* that they experienced in reservation communities.[6]

In the 1950s, the Bureau of Indian Affairs (BIA) began "relocation," moving jobless reservation Indians to jobs in cities. The BIA established relocation offices in Los Angeles, Denver, Salt Lake City, Los Angeles, and Chicago, among other urban areas. The BIA told Indian families that all services on the reservation would be ended and there would be no more aid for them. The idea of relocation was to get the Indians off the reservation and give them work, thus "solving" the Indian problem. Individuals were given a one-way bus ticket to the city, and they received funds from a subsistence program for food and bus fare. Those funds lasted for up to three weeks, supposedly enough time for the Indians to find jobs.

From 1952 to 1972, over one hundred thousand Indians from across the United States relocated. However, many moved back and forth from the reservation and did not hold long-term urban jobs. Many hated city life, finding it alien to reservation culture. Again, the women adapted more easily than the men did and remained the steadying center of the family. Often, they were the ones who found full-time jobs. They gathered with other women as they had at home, but now they joined with women of other tribes.

The BIA tried to use relocation as a way of destroying tribal identity, but the result was not as expected. In a number of cities, the policy created Indian ghettos filled with members of many dissimilar tribes. Within this melting pot, the people began to

A grandmother
holding an infant
in a traditional
cradleboard.
*South Dakota State
Historical Society*

identify ethnically as "Indian" rather than by their tribal affilia-
tions. This pan-Indian concept led to the creation of Indian cen-
ters and organizations such as the American Indian Movement
(AIM) in urban areas.[7] The policy also resulted in mixed-tribal
marriages, but offspring of such unions claimed the mother's reservation as home. Therefore, the tradition of children belonging
to the mother thrived in urban conditions, and the children were
a part of her *tiyospaye.*

Tiyospaye is synonymous with "extended family" and describes
the social organization of tribal members related by blood, marriage, or adoption who lived in one band. Today, *tiyospaye* is
still a valued tradition, but the members often do not reside in
one place, and a person will find kinship in far-flung sites. When

Flora Driving Hawk, Harriet Ross, and the author's daughter, Shirley Sneve, Okreek, South Dakota. *Virginia Driving Hawk Sneve Collection*

I was growing up on the Rosebud reservation during the 1930s and 1940s, families still lived in the prereservation structure. The first home I remember was in Mission, South Dakota, a two-room house next to the home of my grandparents. My great-grandparents lived across the road; down toward the creek lived an aunt and uncle; and other kin resided nearby. This was the traditional *tiyospaye*, and the whole community cherished children.[8]

When Wanbdi Winyan, born in 1896, was orphaned in early childhood, she knew that she was esteemed and loved by her grandparents and the entire tribal *tiyospaye*.[9] This environment survived well into the 1970s, as Delphine Red Shirt wrote in 1998: "I grew up with aunts, uncles, cousins, and various relatives and neighbors who have permeated all that I have become. . . . [They] became a part of my consciousness forever."[10]

As Sioux families increasingly moved from the reservation, related women still tended to find housing or campsites near each other. In Rapid City, Indian families camped near Sioux San and along Rapid Creek, which runs through the city. The disastrous flood of 1972 destroyed many of these sites. Yet, the families found refuge in still-standing homes of other Indians, their *tiyospaye* in the city. A low-income housing area developed in North Rapid called "Sioux Addition," also known as Lakota Homes, even though it was open to all races. In these new communities, the women maintained family connections and had steady employment. They found work as motel or house cleaners and other low-income occupations for unskilled workers. They recognized the need for education of their children so that the next generation could get better paying jobs.[11]

Sioux women also addressed the high Indian student dropout rate in public schools and colleges. Dee LeBeau-Hein of Cheyenne River reservation earned a master's degree at the University of South Dakota in 2001; now, she mentors other Indian students, helping them "navigate the often overwhelming and confusing environment of college campus life, and overcome cultural issues that can cause Native Americans to skip college or give up too soon." Dee continued efforts begun by the University of South Dakota, Black Hills State University, South Dakota State University, and other state colleges that provide on-campus help for Indian students. They offer courses in Native American Studies with a degreed Indian person in charge. Often these programs give counseling services and a sense of *tiyospaye* to homesick students.[12]

Tribes also established colleges on the reservations to encourage Indian students to continue their education. Non-traditional students, more often women, take classes that fit their working

schedules or babysitting needs. In Rapid City, Oglala Lakota College from the Pine Ridge reservation opened a center where many nontraditional Indian students can earn a degree. There are Indian teachers, counselors, and administrator in the Rapid City public schools—just as there are in reservation schools. *Tiyospaye* now takes many forms in many places.[13]

Women, the center of the family circle, continue to keep in touch with *tiyospaye* members all over the nation. My mother, who moved to California and lived to be ninety-nine years old, first wrote letters, telephoned, and later emailed relatives. She visited her reservation-based siblings every other year for as long as she was physically able. She was delighted to find descendants of an uncle in California, her mother's brother who had relocated in the 1950s. His daughter had vanished into a non-Indian world, or so it seemed. Then, one of his granddaughters living in California began searching for her roots and found my mother. This long-lost relative wrote: "My sister and I are very interested in our family. We always thought that there were so few of us, but now we have all of these relatives—we are rich in family."[14] She had found *tiyospaye.*

The circle will never end.

A Sioux matriarch with two granddaughters wearing jingle dresses, 1948. *South Dakota State Historical Society*

CHAPTER 1. WOMEN'S ROLE

1 Another telling of this story can be found in my book *Completing the Circle*, pp. 2-4.

2 Roger Broer, quoted in Deanna Darr, "Exploring the Buffalo Bond," p. 2.

3 One collection of such stories can be found in South Dakota Writer's Project, comp., *Legends of the Mighty Sioux*.

4 Standing Bear, *My People the Sioux*, pp. 7-8.

5 Standing Bear, *My People the Sioux*, pp. 13-20.

6 Powers, *Oglala Women*, pp. 70-71.

7 Swan, *Madonna Swan*, pp. 40-41.

8 Swan, *Madonna Swan*, pp. 41-42.

9 Swan, *Madonna Swan*, p. 43.

10 Sneve, *Completing the Circle*, pp. 101-2.

11 Powers, *Oglala Women*, p. 86.

12 "The Moving Robe Interview" (1931), reprinted in Hardoff, comp. & ed., *Lakota Recollections of the Custer Fight*, pp. 91-96.

13 Eastman, "Rain-in-the-Face," p. 511.

14 "Mary Brave Bird," en.wikipedia.org.

CHAPTER 2. WINTER COUNTS AND CHANGING TIMES

1 Sneve, *Completing the Circle*, pp. 4-18.

2 To read more about Indian women in the fur-trade era, *see* Van Kirk, *Many Tender Ties*.

3 Sneve, *Completing the Circle*, pp. 24-25.

4 Sneve, *Completing the Circle*, pp. 32, 56, 64.

CHAPTER 3. RESERVATION AND SCHOOL

1 Dawes Act, 1887, ourdocuments.gov.

2   Keeble, "Ina, Wanbdi Winyan," p. 10.

3   Sneve, *That They May Have Life*, p. 99; Deloria, *Speaking of Indians*, pp. 8–19.

4   Deloria, *Speaking of Indians*, p. 117.

5   Brown, *Stubborn Fool*, pp. 45–46.

6   Sneve, *That They May Have Life*, pp. 6–7.

7   This story was originally published in a different form as "First Christmas," in *Returning the Gift*, ed. Bruchac, pp. 265–67.

CHAPTER 4. WOMEN ADAPT

1   Red Shirt, *Bead on an Anthill*, pp. 136–37.

2   *See BishopAccountability.org*, www.bishop-accountability.org.

3   Paulson and Moses, *Who's Who among the Sioux*, p. 6.

4   Chapman, *Remember the Wind*, dust-jacket copy.

5   Chapman, *Remember the Wind*, p. 69.

6   Quoted from a school circular in Sneve, *That They May Have Life*, p. 102.

7   Sneve, *Completing the Circle*, p. 66.

8   Riggs, *Early Days at Santee*, p. 50.

9   Sneve, *Completing the Circle*, p. 66.

10 [Eastman], "Indian Girls in Indian Schools," p. 201.

11 Zitkala-Sa, *American Indian Stories*, p. 69.

12 Roseann Hoefel, "Zitkala-Sa: A Biography." *See also* Rappaport, *Flight of Red Bird*, intro., and Zitkala-Sa, *Dreams and Thunder*, ed. Hafen, pp. xiii–xxiv.

13 "Ella Cara Deloria," *Voices from the Gaps*, conservancy.umn.edu; Agnes Picotte, "Biographical Sketch of the Author," in Deloria, *Waterlily*, pp. 229–31.

14 [Ross], *Keeper of the Female Medicine Bundle*, pp. i, iv, 11–14.

15 [Ross], *Keeper of the Female Medicine Bundle*, p. iv; Paulson and Moses, *Who's Who among the Sioux*, pp. 203–4.

16 Paulson and Moses, *Who's Who among the Sioux*, p. 18.

17. Paulson and Moses, *Who's Who among the Sioux*, p. 81; Weinberg, *The Real Rosebud*, pp. 28, 32–37, 42–44.

18 Paulson and Moses, *Who's Who among the Sioux*, p. 265; Weinberg, *The Real Rosebud*, pp. 52–53.

19 Powers, *Oglala Women*, p. 113.

20 Quoted in Lewis, *Wo'wakita Reservation Recollections*, p. 264.

21 Paulson and Moses, *Who's Who among the Sioux*, p. 27; "Zelda C. Gallegos," *Rapid City Journal*, Nov. 24, 2013; "Biography," *JoAnne Bird Art*.

22 Paulson and Moses, *Who's Who among the Sioux*, pp. 10, 127; Eagle, "*Native Sun News*"; [Ross], *Keeper of the Female Medicine Bundle*, p. iv.

23 Quoted in Barari, "The Awakening."

24 "Elizabeth Cook-Lynn," *Voices from the Gaps*, conservancy. umn.edu.

25 "Report Addresses Public Safety Gaps Found on Reservations."

26 Ybanez, "The Evolution of Domestic Violence and Reform Efforts across Indian Country."

27 Powers, *Oglala Women*, p. 173.

28 Quoted in Powers, *Oglala Women*, p. 177.

29 "Facts about FASDs," *Center for Disease Control and Prevention*, cdc.gov.

30 *White Buffalo Calf Woman Society*, wbcws.org.

CHAPTER 5. THE CIRCLE NEVER ENDS

1 Powers, *Oglala Women*, pp. 120–21.

2 Red Shirt, *Bead on an Anthill*, pp. 35–36.

3 A fictionalized version of this story appears in my book *Lana's Lakota Moons*, pp. 35–36.

4 Quoted in Gesick, "Dance Program Honors Heritage," *Rapid City Journal*, Dec. 5, 2013.

5 Powers, *Oglala Women*, p. 125.

6 Sneve, "Tiyospaye," p. 505.

7   "American Indian Relocation," *Native American Netroots*, nativeamericannetroots.net.

8   Sneve, "Tiyospaye," pp. 500, 505.

9   Keeble, "Ina, Wanbdi Winyan," p. 10.

10   Red Shirt, *Bead on an Anthill*, p. 9.

11   Sneve, "Tiyospaye," p. 505.

12   Gesick, "Program Breaks Down Barriers."

13   Sneve, "Tiyospaye," pp. 505–6.

14   Roberta Fitzsimmons, Stockton, Calif., email to author, Dec. 21, 2002.

BOOKS AND ARTICLES

Barari, Molly. "The Awakening." *Rapid City Journal*, Nov. 17, 2013.

Brave Bird, Mary, with Richard Erdoes. *Ohitika Woman*. New York: Grove Press, 1993.

Brown, Estelle Aubrey. *Stubborn Fool: A Narrative*. Caldwell, Idaho: Caxton Printers, 1952.

Chapman, William McK. *Remember the Wind: A Prairie Memoir*. Philadelphia: J. P. Lippincott Co., 1965.

Crow Dog, Mary, and Richard Erdoes. *Lakota Woman*. New York: Grove Weidenfeld, 1990.

Darr, Deanna. "Exploring the Buffalo Bond." *Black Hills to Go*, Dec. 12, 2013.

Deloria, Ella Cara. *Dakota Texts*. Publications of the American Ethnological Society, vol. 14. New York, 1932.

_____. *Speaking of Indians*. New York: Friendship Press, 1944.

_____. *Waterlily*. Lincoln: University of Nebraska Press, 1988.

Eagle, Karin. "*Native Sun News*: Crow Creek Sioux Woman Earns Bronze Star." *Indianz.com*, Dec. 1, 2011.

Eastman, Charles A. "Rain-in-the-Face: The Story of a Sioux Warrior." *The Outlook* 84 (Oct. 27, 1906): 507–12.

[Eastman], Elaine Goodale. "Indian Girls in Indian Schools." *The Home-Maker* 6 (June 1891): 199–205.

Gesick, Jennifer Naylor. "Dance Program Honors Heritage." *Rapid City Journal*, Dec. 5, 2013.

_____. "Program Breaks Down Barriers to Advanced Degrees." *Rapid City Journal*, Dec. 8, 2013.

Hardorff, Richard D., comp. & ed. *Lakota Recollections of the Custer Fight: New Sources of Indian-Military History*. Lincoln: University of Nebraska Press, Bison Books, 1997.

Hoefel, Roseanne. "Zitkala-Sa: A Biography." *The Online Archive of Nineteenth Century U.S. Women's Writings*. Ed. Glynis Carr. www.facstaff.bucknell.edu/gcarr.

Keeble, Blossom. "Ina, Wanbdi Winyan (Mother—the Royal War Eagle Woman)." *Ikce Wicasta: The Common People Journal* 4 (Spring 2001): 8–11.

Lewis, Emily H. *Wo'wakita Reservation Recollections: A People's History of the Allen Issue Station on the Pine Ridge Indian Reservation of South Dakota*. Sioux Falls, S.Dak.: Center for Western Studies, Augustana College, 1980.

Paulson, T. Emogene. *Sioux Collections*. Vermillion: University of South Dakota, 1982.

_____, and Lloyd R. Moses. *Who's Who among the Sioux*. Vermillion: Institute of Indian Studies, University of South Dakota, 1988.

Powers, Marla N. *Oglala Women: Myth, Ritual, and Reality*. Chicago: University of Chicago Press, 1988.

Rappaport, Doreen. *The Flight of Red Bird: The Life of Zitkala-Sa*. New York: Dial Books, 1997.

Red Shirt, Delphine. *Bead on an Anthill: A Lakota Childhood*. Lincoln: University of Nebraska Press, 1998.

"Report Addresses Public Safety Gaps Found on Reservations." *Rapid City Journal*, Nov. 13, 2013.

Riggs, Mary B. *Early Days at Santee: The Beginnings of Santee Normal Training School*. Santee, Nebr.: Santee N.T.S. Press, 1928.

[Ross, Allen]. *Keeper of the Female Medicine Bundle: Biography of Wihopa*. Denver, Colo.: Wiconi Waste Publishing, 1998.

Sneve, Virginia Driving Hawk. *Completing the Circle*. Lincoln: University of Nebraska Press, 1995.

_____. "First Christmas." In *Returning the Gift: Poetry and Prose from the First North American Native Writers' Festival*. Ed. Joseph Bruchac. Tucson: University of Arizona Press, 1994. Pp. 265–67.

_____. *Lana's Lakota Moons*. Lincoln: University of Nebraska Press, 2007.

_____. *That They May Have Life: The Episcopal Church in South Dakota, 1859–1976*. New York: Seabury Press, 1977.

_____. "Tiyospaye: A Traditional Sioux Family Today." In *A New South Dakota History*. Ed. Harry F. Thompson. Sioux Falls, S.Dak.: Center for Western Studies, Augustana College, 2005. Pp. 499–206.

Standing Bear, Luther. *My People the Sioux*. Boston: Houghton Mifflin Co., 1928.

Swan, Madonna. *Madonna Swan: A Lakota Woman's Story*. As told through Mark St. Pierre. Norman: University of Oklahoma Press, 1991.

Van Kirk, Sylvia. *Many Tender Ties: Women in Fur-Trade Society, 1670–1870*. Norman: University of Oklahoma Press, 1980.

Waggoner, Josephine. *Witness: A Húnkpapȟa Historian's Strong-Heart Song of the Lakotas*. Ed. Emily Levine. Lincoln: University of Nebraska Press, 2013.

Weinberg, Marjorie. *The Real Rosebud: The Triumph of a Lakota Woman*. Lincoln: University of Nebraska Press, 2004.

Ybanez, Vicki. "The Evolution of Domestic Violence and Reform Efforts across Indian Country." *Praxis International*, 2002. files.praxisinternational.org.

Zitkala-Sa. *American Indian Stories*. Washington, D.C.: Hayworth Publishing House, 1921.

_____. *Dreams and Thunder: Stories, Poems, and* The Sun Dance Opera. Ed. P. Jane Hafen. Lincoln: University of Nebraska Press, 2001.

"Zelda C. Gallegos." *Rapid City Journal*, Nov. 24, 2013.

INTERNET SITES
BishopAccountabily.org. bishop-accountability.org.
Center for Disease Control and Prevention. cdc.gov.
JoAnne Bird Art. joannebird.com.

Native American Netroots. nativeamericannetroots.net.
Our Documents. ourdocuments.gov.
Voices from the Gaps. conservancy.umn.edu.
White Buffalo Calf Woman Society. wbcws.org.

FILMS

Lakota Woman: Siege at Wounded Knee. TNT, 1994.
Urban Rez. Rocky Mountain [Colorado] PBS, 2013.
Young Lakota. Incite Pictures/Cine Qua Non, 2013.

Numbers in italics refer to illustrations.

Abortion, 68–69

Abuse: at boarding schools, 51, 53; depicted in winter count, 21; drug- and alcohol-related, 70–72; protection of White Buffalo Calf Woman, 5; protection within the *tiyospaye*, 69–70; rape, 26, 69

Acculturation, 26, 28, 55, 63

Activism, 19, 59, 63, 69, 83

Afghanistan, 66, *68*

Album of the American Indian, 63

Alcohol, 25–26, 70–71

Allotment, 26, 29

All Saints School, 59, 61

American Indian Movement (AIM), 19–20, 83

Anog Ite (Double-Faced Woman), 8–9

Archambault, Marie Therese, 53

Ashley, Rose, 66

The Atlantic Monthly, 59

Augustana College, 1

Battle of the Little Bighorn, 19, 26

Bdi Bdi Win (Evelyn Dumarce Crawford), 29

Beadwork: and clothing, 28, 73; as collectibles, 33; learning and teaching of, 14, 72; origins, 13; as source of income, 56, 63, 66

Bergen, Evelyn Lambert, 61

Bird, Jackie, 66

Bird, Joanne, 66

Blue Legs, Alice, 66

Boarding schools: attendance requirement, 28–29, 42; chores, 31–33; church and religious instruction, 38, 40; clash with Indian culture and values, 29–30, 36, 42, 54, 59; clothing, sewing, and laundry, 31–35, *36*; cooking, food, and meals, 31, 40, 51; and cultural destruction, 72; discipline and student abuse, 51, 53; English and Indian languages in, 33, 40; Episcopal, 40, 51, 53; gender separation, 17, 33, 36, 40, 43; music and student drill, 35–36; Presbyterian, 40, 51; Quaker, 51, 57; recollection of Christmas at, 42–50; replaced by day schools, 57; replaced by public schools, 73, 85; Roman Catholic, 40, 51; sneaking out at night, 54–55

Boas, Franz, 59

Bonnin, Gertrude, 57–59

Bonnin, Ray, 57

Buffalo, 6, *12*, 13, 56

Buffalo Bill's Wild West, 62

Buffalo Ceremony, 15

Bureau of Indian Affairs (BIA), 19, 29, 61, 82

Burt, Mr. and Mrs., 43, 47–48

Cante T'inza (Strong Heart) Society, 19

Carleton College, 61

Carlisle Indian School, 10–11, 51–52, 59

Ceremonies and rituals: Buffalo Ceremony, 15; giveaways, 76–77, 80; medicine men, 17; and menstruation, 13–15; sun dance, 68, 73; use of the pipe for healing, 6; vision quest, 47, 68

Chapman, William McK., 54

Cheyenne River Indian Reservation, 40

Childbirth, 5–6, 21, 25, 47

Christianity: and Indian conversion, 28, 48, 53, 55–56; school celebration of Christmas,

42–50. *See also* Boarding schools

Circles: as concept in Sioux life, 1–2; women as the center of, 87. *See also Tiyospaye*

Citizenship, 35, 59

Clifford, Serena, 68–69

Completing the Circle, 2, 10

Cook-Lynn, Elizabeth, 69

Coolidge, Calvin, 62

Courtship. *See* Marriage

Crafts: beadwork, 13–14, 28, 33, 56, 63, 66, 72–73; dolls, 63, 66; quillwork, 8–10, 13, 28, 33, 56, 66; teaching, 63

Crawford, Evelyn Dumarce, 29

Crawler, Mary, *18*, 19, 26

Crow Creek Indian Reservation, 40

Crow Dog, Mary, 19

Custer, George Armstrong, 19

Dakota Grammar, 59

Dakota Sioux Indians, 1, 3

Dakota Texts, 59

Dances, 62, 66, 68. *See also* Powwows

Dawes Act (1887), 26, 29

Deloria, Ella Cara, 30, *31*, 59

Deloria, Philip, 59

Deloria, Vine, 59

De Smet, Pierre, 28

Divorce, 70

Drifting Goose (Sioux Indian), 47–48

Driving Hawk, Flora, *16*, *49*, *84*; attends school, 54; courtship, 17; recollections, 31, 42–43; storytelling, 3–6, 72

Driving Hawk, James, *49*

Driving Hawk, Robert, 17, *49*, 50, 54

Earlham College, 59

Eastman, Elaine Goodale, 56

Erdoes, Richard, 20

Family. *See Tiyospaye*

Fetal alcohol syndrome, 70–71

Fire Thunder, Cecilia, 68–69

Flandreau Indian Reservation, 40, 61

Flandreau Indian School, *32*, *44*, 66

Flood, Elsie, 63, 66

Frazier, Hannah, *2*

Fur-trading era, 23, 25

Gallegos, Zelda, 66

Gender: roles in Sioux society, 3; separation of sexes at boarding school, 17, 33, 36, 40, 43; and White Buffalo Calf Woman, 5–6

General Allotment Act (1887), 26, 29

Giveaways, 76–77, 80

Gonzalez, Mario, 69

Grandfathers, 14

Grandmothers: importance of, 2, 6; as keepers of the medicine bundle, 61; role in the family, 14–15, 71–72, 80; storytelling, 3, 6, 8, 10; teaching skills and values, 63, 66, 72, 76; and transition to reservation life, 29. *See also Tiyospaye*

Grant, Ulysses S., 40

Great Sioux Reservation, 26

Griffith, Stephanie R., 66, *68*

Hampton Institute, 51

Hanwi (the moon), 9, 14

Hare, William H., 54

Harper's, 59

Hayes, Delores, 76
Hennepin, Louis, 28
Holy Rosary Mission, 51
Homosexuality, 9-10
Hutson, Thisbe, *30*

Indian Citizenship Act (1924), 59

Jingle dance and dresses, 76, *78-79*
Jones Beach Indian Village, 62

Korean Conflict, 66
Koupal, Nancy Tystad, 1

Lakota Sioux Indians, 1, 3
Lakota Woman, 20
Land allotment, 26, 29
LeBeau, Marcella, 66, *67*
Loafer band, 25
Lower Brule Indian Reservation, 17
Lower Cut Meat School, *37*

Madonna Swan, 14-15
Maka Ina (Mother Earth), 14
Marriage: and adultery, 23; and Christianity, 28; and courting practices, 17; divorce, 70; and initiation ceremony, 15; plural marriage, 6, 23, 25; premarital sex, 6, 13; and White Buffalo Calf Woman, 5-6; with whites, 23, 25, 61-62
Medicine bundles, 5, 61
Medicine men and women, 16-17, 19
Menstruation and initiation ceremonies, 13-15
Mission, S.Dak., 54
Missionaries: cultural changes imposed by, 28;

and misunderstandings of Indian culture, 3; organizing women's societies, 55-56; presence on reservations, 40
Moving Robe Woman (Mary Crawler), *18*, 19, 26
My People the Sioux, 10-11

Nakota Sioux Indians, 1, 3
Napešni (No Flight) Society, 19
Native American Committee, 63
Newberry Library, 63
Nordland Fest, 1

Oberlin College, 59
Oglala Lakota College, 87
Ohitika Win (Mary Crow Dog), 19
Ohitika Woman, 20
Ojibwa Indians, 1
Old Indian Legends, 59
Oral tradition: legend of Anog Ite, 8-9; legend of White Buffalo Calf Woman, 3-6, 14; role in Sioux culture, 6, 10; teaching grandchildren by, 72; and transmission of legends, 62-63. *See also* Winter counts
Pehin Hanska (George Armstrong Custer), 19
Pejuta Okawin, 16-17
Pierre Indian School, *38*
Pine Ridge Boarding School, *41*
Pine Ridge Day School No. 29, *34*
Pine Ridge Indian Reservation, *30*, *39*, 40, 51, 87
Pipes. *See* sacred pipes
The Politics of Hallowed Ground, 69
Posey, Rose Driving Hawk, 2
Powers, Marla, 63, 69
Powwows: and female dancers, 73-76; and giveaways, 76-77, 80; jingle dance and

dresses, 76, *78–79*; and male dancers, 73; meaning of, 73; trilling and drumming, 17, 73, 76, 80. *See also* Dances

Pretty Face (Sioux Indian), 12–13

Prostitution, 26, 28, 70

Quillwork, 8–10, 13, 28, 33, 56, 66

Quilting, 2, 56, 72, 77. *See also* Star quilts

Racial discrimination, 69

Radisson, Pierre, 3

Rain-in-the-Face (Sioux Indian), 19

Rape, 26, 29

Rapid City, S.Dak., 62, 69, 81–82, 84, 87

Rapid City Journal, 69, 76

Rations, 28–29, 42

Red Cloud Indian School, 51

Red Shirt, Delphine, 51, 73, *77*, 84–85

Religion. *See* Boarding Schools; Christianity; Missionaries

Rickers, Bonita, *79*

Riggs, Mary, 56

Rituals. *See* Ceremonies and rituals

Rohay, Bette, *67*

Roman Catholic church: and boarding schools, 40, 51; early missionary presence, 28; sexual abuse of children, 51, 53

"Romancing the West," 1

Roosevelt, Franklin D., 59

Rosebud Indian Reservation, *35*, 40, 51, *53*, 54, 72

Ross, Agnes, 59–61, 68

Ross, Harriet, 2, *84*

Ross, Harvey, *60*, 61

Ross, Olive, 66

Sacred bundles, 5, 61

Sacred circles, 80. *See also* Powwows

Sacred pipes, 5–6, 14, 48

Saint Elizabeth's School for Indian Boys and Girls, 54

Saint Francis Indian School, 51

Saint Mary's Episcopal School, *35*, *53*, 54

Santee Sioux Indians, 3, 61

Sexual abuse. *See* Abuse

Sioux Indians: bands and tribal divisions, 3, 25; gender roles, 3, 6; origin of name, 1; and *tiyospaye*, 80–87; winter counts, 20–23

Sisseton Indian Reservation, 40

Skan (spirit of the sky), 9

Sneve, Virginia Driving Hawk: at age sixteen, 2; attends St. Mary's school, 54–55; storytelling, 72

Snyder Act (1924), 59

Speaking of Indians, 59

Standing Bear, Luther, 10–13, 62

Standing Cloud (Santee Sioux Indian), 61

Standing Rock Indian Reservation, 40, 54

Star quilts, 2, *55*, 77. *See also* Quilting

Storytelling: legend of Anog Ite, 8–9; legend of White Buffalo Calf Woman, 3–6, 14; role in Sioux culture, 6, 10; teaching grandchildren by, 72; and transmission of legends, 62–63. *See also* Winter counts

St. Pierre, Mark, 14

Suicide, 21, 23

Sun dance, 68, 73

Swan, Madonna, *13*, 14–15

Tate (spirit of the wind), 9, 14

Teton Sioux Indians, 3

Tipis: ceremonial, *24*; for councils, 4–5; ownership of, 6; preparing and decorating, 13; replaced, 28–29, 56–57

Tiyospaye (extended family): and childcare, 80; community support from, 30, 80, 85; losing the closeness of, 56, 82; meaning of, 83–85; non-traditional forms, 85, 87; and reservation life, 25–26. *See also* Grandmothers

Tokala (Fox) Society, 19

Tonweya and the Eagles, 63

Trail of Broken Treaties, 19

Trilling, 17, 73

University of South Dakota, 63

Vietnam War, 66

Violence. *See* Abuse

Violence against Women Act of 1994, 69

Vision quests, 47, 68

Wacipi. See Powwows

Wahpeton Indian School, 64–65

Wakantanka (the Great Spirit), 4–5

War, 17, 19–20, 66–68

Warrior societies, 17, 19

Waterlily, 59

Weston, Andrew, 42

White Buffalo Calf Woman, 3–6, 10, 14, 72

White Buffalo Calf Woman Society, 72

White Horse, Lee, 63

White settlement, 25–26

White's Manual Institute, 51, 57

Whope. *See* White Buffalo Calf Woman

Why I Can't Read Wallace Stegner and Other Essays, 69

Wi (sun god), 9

Wicazo Sa Review, 69

Wihopa (Agnes Ross), 59–61, 68

Winter counts, 20–23. *See also* Oral tradition

Winyan omniciye (women's societies), 53, 55–56

"The Women of the Circle," 1

World War II, 61, 66–67, 70, 81

Wounded Knee, S.Dak., 19–20

Yankton Indian Reservation, 40, 57

Yankton Sioux Indians, 3, 61

Yellow Robe, Chauncey, 62

Yellow Robe, Chauncina, 63

Yellow Robe, Evelyn, 63

Yellow Robe, Rosebud, 62–63

Young Lakota (documentary film), 69

Zitkala-Sa (Gertrude Bonnin), 57–59